GLUTEN-FREE WARRIOR

GLUTEN-FREE & WHEAT-FREE WHOLE FOODS RECIPES

GENEVIEVE SHERROW, MS, CN

For my family: Pauline, Joanne, Lionel and Nellie

Warrior Contents

Acknowledgements

Collaborative efforts have made the evolution of this cookbook possible. First and foremost, I would like to thank my older sister Joanne Sherrow for giving me the motivation to put this book out into the world. I thank my younger sister Pauline Sherrow for her genius work on the book cover design, and for her emotional support. My mother and father gave me an abundance of support and resources while I was in graduate school, and I am indebted to them for the sacrifices that they made to make that possible. I thank my mother for her strength, resilience and generosity. I am grateful for my family, friends, colleagues and former classmates who tested and tasted the recipes in this book: Jared Rice, Katrina Olson, Gabe Ehri, Bonnie Ehri, Keri Romerdahl, Bill Gregory, Kristina Alnajjar, Kate Murray, Jenna Umbriac, Theresa Bliffert, Dr. Cristen Harris, Amy Sellers, Katie Lake, Brian Hutchinson, Christy Baker-Smith, Julie Miller, Mary Purdy, Angie Waco, Liz Knaster, Barry Brummit, Maja Zavaljevski, Kelly Borchert, Erin Asales, Arika Dortero, Danielle Holliday, Kellyn Milani, Lauren Ellis, Kim Humphrey, Allegra Hart. I must thank Elizabeth Melton, Victor Guy, Ivy and Layla Melton for their kindness, warmth and support during my transition back east. They worked tirelessly to publicize my book launch party. I express gratitude for the inspiration for this book which came from my classmates and professors at Bastyr University. Among them are Cynthia Lair, Jennifer Adler, Nick Rose, Boonchai Apichai, Kathleen Lumiere, Theresa Bliffert, Jared Rice, Sonja Max and Amy Adams. Cynthia Lair, one of my culinary instructors at Bastyr University, reviewed and edited several of my recipes and my book proposal. I thank her for her kindness, patience and willingness to help me. When I began writing about gluten-free diets and nutrition at Bastyr, Elizabeth Kirk, my professor and mentor from Bastyr, supported me through my writing process with patience and a gentle spirit. During that time, I was able to build up a substantive writing portfolio, a blog and the beginnings of this book. I also had an opportunity to work with Dr. Stephen Wangen and Cynthia Kupper in Seattle and I value their work in the national celiac disease and gluten intolerance community. To the National Foundation for Celiac Awareness in Philadelphia, I hope to build long lasting relationships with your staff members and your community. I look forward to forging new relationships with individuals in the gluten intolerance and celiac disease communities in the Northeast and beyond. Finally, I thank all of my future readers who find this book to be their go-to resource for whole foods gluten-free and wheat-free cooking.

Introduction

In September, 2007, I discovered I was intolerant to gluten after doing what nutritionists call an elimination challenge diet protocol. I removed gluten from my diet for two weeks and when I reintroduced it, I had a severe digestive reaction. Throughout most of my life, I never felt particularly well after eating a gluten-heavy meal, though I never associated my digestive symptoms with a food intolerance. Luckily, when I was diagnosed, I had just began a graduate program in nutrition at a natural medicine university in Seattle, Bastyr University, and I was surrounded by alternative health care practitioners and immersed in an environment of holistic nutrition. I was fortunate to have access to nutritional and medical resources that don't exist in many areas of the country.

One of the most challenging aspects of the gluten-free diet is accessing gluten-free food options and solid resources for cooking. Bastyr University's vegetarian cafeteria always had gluten-free food options and Seattle is one of those areas of the country that is very aware of gluten intolerance. Gluten-free food is readily available in most food stores and restaurants.

Inspiration from my nutrition graduate program motivated me to write this book. First, the nutrition curriculum at Bastyr is grounded in the therapeutic applications of whole foods nutrition. Some of the most inspirational courses I completed at Bastyr that influenced the material in this book include: Traditional Chinese Medicine Therapeutic Nutrition and Cooking, Ayurvedic Nutrition and Cooking, Whole Foods Production, Therapeutic Whole Foods Cooking and Bioactive Compounds in Foods. Many of my classmates had been chefs in their former careers and their culinary tendencies inspired me to try new foods and cooking methods. While I was in Seattle, I also took advantage of opportunities to go on seaweed harvesting expeditions in Washington's San Juan Islands, and learned a tremendous amount about the medicinal value of sea vegetables and their culinary applications.

What I learned about cooking while I was in graduate school was that whole foods cooking inspired by ethnic cuisine was the key to a satisfying and enjoyable gluten-free diet. I am particularly drawn to Indian and East Asian cuisines because I adore food that has complex, rich flavors and spices. I am also drawn to the medicinal and therapeutic qualities of certain foods that are used in those cultures.

Gluten-free Warrior is not just for those on a gluten-free diet, it is for people who choose to eat a healthfully, the whole foods way, free of gluten and wheat. It is my hope that *Gluten-free Warrior* becomes the answer to your desire for satisfying and flavorful gluten-free meals. All of the recipes in this book are original. They are suitable for adults and children, and can be prepared anytime of the day. Try them and they will undoubtedly unleash the warrior inside you.

Genevieve Sherrow
December, 2010

MORNING NOURISHMENT

Nutty Millet Porridge
Triple Grain Cereal
Scallion, Walnut, Nori Scramble
The Blue-est Muffins
Honey Butter Corn Grits
Banana Nut Pancakes
Cream of Tef with Dates and Honey
Oat Hazelnut Porridge
Asian Breakfast Rice
The Blue-est Corncakes
Creamy Buckwheat Porridge

Nutty Millet Porridge

Millet is a high protein, whole grain. Allergen-free and great for special diets, this nutty, sweet hot breakfast cereal will nourish you on a cold winter morning.

1/2 cup dry hulled millet
2 1/2 cups water
Pinch of sea salt
1/2 teaspoon sesame seeds
1 tablespoon sunflower seeds, crushed
2 teaspoons butter or ghee
2 tablespoons maple syrup
1/8 cup of dried fruit (cranberries, raisins, or currants)
Variation: substitute 1/4 teaspoon nutritional yeast for maple syrup

Heat a dry pot to medium. Add millet. Stir grain with a wooden spoon. After a few minutes the grains will begin to pop and give off a nutty aroma. Add water and salt. Bring to a boil. Simmer for approximately 20 minutes, stirring occasionally. Millet will soften like a porridge. Stir in sesame and sunflower seeds. Add butter and maple syrup. Taste and adjust salt or syrup. Ladle into your favorite breakfast bowl. Top with dried fruit of your choice.

Preparation time: 20 minutes
Makes 1-2 servings

Triple Grain Cereal

1/2 cup rice
1/2 cup millet
1/2 cup quinoa
3 cups water

Rinse and drain all grains and nuts/seeds in a fine strainer. Toast grains (millet, rice, quinoa) in one of two ways:

Oven toasting:
Preheat oven to 350 F. Spread grains on a cookie sheet and toast in oven until they give off a nutty aroma (12-15 minutes).

Skillet toasting:
Place washed grains in a large skillet on burner and toast on medium heat, stirring constantly, until grains give off a nutty aroma (5 - 8 minutes).

Let grains cool for about 5 minutes. Grind grains just prior to using in a small electric grinder, coffee grinder or food processor. Combine ground grains and 3 cups water in a pot; bring to a boil. Reduce heat to low and simmer, covered, for 10-12 minutes.

Top plain cooked cereal with a little maple syrup, nut or rice milk and fruit.

Preparation time: 25 minutes
Makes 3 servings

Scallion, Walnut and Nori Scramble

Nori, a sea vegetable, is often used for rolling sushi. Nori provides an abundance of vitamins and minerals, a source of salt and abundant flavor. Try crushed nori in your egg scrambles. This dish is perfect for breakfast, brunch or even a quick dinner.

2 teaspoons butter
3 green onions, chopped
2 cloves fresh garlic, minced
4 eggs, beaten
2 dried nori sheets, crushed and torn into small pieces
2 tablespoons walnuts or raw cashews, chopped
Sea salt and crushed black pepper to taste

Heat skillet to medium-high, add butter. Sauté green onion and garlic for 1 minute. Add eggs and scramble. Crush and tear nori sheets into small pieces and fold into eggs. Nori should soften as it combines with the eggs. Add walnuts and remove from heat. Taste and adjust salt and pepper as needed.

Preparation time: 8 minutes
Makes 2 servings

The Blue-est Muffins

My friend and colleague Amy Adams adapted this recipe from Karen Robertson's gluten-free cooking bible *Cooking Gluten-Free.* These muffins are moist and tender. Serve them for brunch or as a snack. They are sure to wow your gluten-free and non-gluten-free comrades.

1 cup blue corn meal (yellow corn meal can also be used)
1/2 cup Bob's Red Mill all-purpose gluten-free flour blend
1/2 cup succanat or brown sugar
1/2 teaspoon baking soda
1/2 teaspoon baking powder
1/2 teaspoon salt
2 eggs
1 cup whole milk plain yogurt, kefir, or buttermilk
1/2 teaspoon lemon extract or lemon zest
1 cup fresh blueberries, frozen will do when out of season (for blueberry lovers add and additional 1/2 cup)

Preheat oven to 350 degrees. Combine dry ingredients in mixing bowl. Add egg, milk, and lemon. Stir until mixture is smooth. Fold in blueberries. Spoon into greased muffins trays. Bake at 350 for approximately 15 minutes.

Preparation time: 30 minutes
Makes 12 medium size muffins

Adapted by Amy Adams and Genevieve Sherrow from Karen Robertson's, *Cooking Gluten-Free.*

Honey Butter Corn Grits

1 cup polenta, medium grain or corn grits, dry
4 cups water
1/2 teaspoon salt
2 tablespoons butter
3 tablespoons honey
1/4 cup dried cranberries
Note: Cornmeal cannot be used in this recipe

Combine polenta, water and salt in pot and bring to boil. Reduce heat to low and simmer for about 45 minutes. Stir frequently, every 10 minutes or so. Mid-way through cooking add butter and stir. Add honey towards the end of cooking. Consistency of polenta should be soft and thick when cooked. Taste and adjust salt and sweetener. Serve hot in breakfast bowls and top off with cranberries.

Preparation time: 50 minutes
Makes 4 servings

Banana Nut Pancakes

This recipe will satisfy your cravings for that occasional pancake breakfast. Low in sugar, high in fiber and egg-free; it will become your pancake go-to.

1 1/2 cups buckwheat flour
1/2 cup ground cashews (use a blender or food processor)
1/4 teaspoon sea salt
1 teaspoon baking powder
1 tablespoon honey or rice syrup
1 1/4 cups milk, rice, nut or cow
2 tablespoons canola or safflower oil
1 banana, mashed

Combine flour, cashews, salt and baking powder in a medium bowl and set aside. Combine sweetener, milk, oil and banana in a small bowl; mix thoroughly and lightly stir into dry ingredients.

Heat non-stick skillet or griddle to medium- high. Drop pancake batter by tablespoon onto pan surface. When brown and bubbly, turn. As batter thickens, add water, a tablespoon at a time, to keep cakes thin.

Serve warm on a weekend morning with maple syrup or fruit jam of choice.

Preparation time: 20 minutes
Makes about 12 medium-size pancakes (4 inches in diameter)

Cream of Tef with Dates and Honey

If you've dined in Ethiopian restaurants, you've had Tef. Ingera, the flat bread served with food, is made from Tef flour. Native to Ethiopian cultures, Tef is a miniscule brown grain which is nutritionally superior to other grains because of its high mineral content. When cooked like porridge and mixed with milk and sweet honey, this is a breakfast you won't skip in the morning.

1/4 cup whole grain tef
2 cups water
Pinch sea salt
1/2 cup medjool dates, chopped
1 tablespoon honey
Milk of choice (rice, nut, cow)

Toast tef in dry saucepan over medium heat until it emits a fragrant aroma, about 2-3 minutes. Add water and salt and bring to a boil, stirring constantly. Reduce heat and simmer covered for about 5 minutes, stirring occasionally. Stir in dates and honey. Serve hot with milk of choice.

Preparation time: 10 minutes
Makes 1-2 servings

Recipe adapted by Genevieve Sherrow with inspiration from Rebecca Wood's *The Splendid Grain.*

Oat Hazelnut Porridge

1/2 cup steel cut oats, dry
2 1/4 cups water
Pinch of sea salt
1 tablespoon maple syrup, brown sugar or succanat
1/4 cup roasted hazelnuts, crushed
1 tablespoon dried cranberries, currants or raisins
Dash of cinnamon
Optional: 1 tablespoon milk, rice, soy or cow

Combine oats and water in a mixing bowl and soak overnight. Transfer oats and soaking water into a pot with salt. Bring to a boil. Be sure to watch the oats otherwise they will boil over the top of the pot. Simmer for approximately 20-25 minutes, stirring occasionally. Oats will soften like porridge.

Ladle into your favorite breakfast bowl. Add syrup or brown sugar. Top with hazelnuts, dried fruit and cinnamon. If oats are too stiff, add milk to soften.

Preparation time: 30 minutes
Serves: 1-2

Asian Breakfast Rice

Try something different for breakfast! This tasty dish has all the ingredients for getting your day off to a healthy start. Throw it in the fridge and save some for lunch or dinner.

1 cup basmati brown or white rice, dry
2 cups water
1 tablespoon unrefined, extra-virgin olive oil
3 shittake mushrooms, sliced thinly
2 dried nori sheets, crushed or torn
2 tablespoons toasted sesame oil
4 tablespoons wheat-free tamari (San-J or Eden Brand)
1 teaspoon black or white sesame seeds
1/2 cup roasted almonds or cashews, crushed
Sea salt to taste

Combine rice and water in pot, cover and bring to boil. Reduce heat to low and simmer for 25-30 minutes or until all of the water has absorbed. Do not stir or agitate rice during cooking. Tilt pot gently to a 45-degree angle to see whether water has been absorbed. Let rice cool for 10 minutes.

Heat skillet to medium-high, then add olive oil. Saute mushrooms for about 2 minutes. Add cooked rice and crushed nori to mushrooms and stir. Coat mixture with sesame oil and soy sauce. Top with sesame seeds and nuts. Taste and adjust salt as needed. Serve warm with a cup of ginger tea.

Preparation time: Approximately 40 minutes or 15 minutes if next day rice is used
Makes 3 servings

The Blue-est Corn Cakes

1 cup blue corn meal (I use Arrowhead Mills GF brand)
1/4 cup Bob's Red Mill GF Flour Blend
Pinch of sea salt
1/4 teaspoon baking powder
1 egg, beaten
1 tablespoon olive oil or canola oil
3/4 cup rice milk (soy, nut or cow's milk can also be used)
1 tablespoon raw honey
1/4 teaspoon raw sesame seeds
1 teaspoon butter, for frying
Optional: 1 tablespoon blackberry or blueberry jam

Combine all dry ingredients in a mixing bowl. Add egg, oil, milk and honey (in that order) to dry ingredients and mix thoroughly. Batter should have a thicker consistency. Fold in sesame seeds.

Heat skillet to medium-high, add butter. Drop pancake batter by tablespoon onto skillet. Brown on both sides. Serve warm with jam.

Preparation time: 15 minutes
Makes: about 8 pancakes

Creamy Buckwheat Porridge

1 cup raw buckwheat groats, dry
4 cups water
1/4 teaspoon sea salt
1/2 cup milk
4 tablespoons maple syrup
Sea salt to taste

Soak buckwheat groats in 4 cups of water overnight. Pour buckwheat, soaking water and 1/4 teaspoon of salt into a medium saucepan and bring to a boil. Immediately reduce heat to low and simmer for about 20-25 minutes or until all of the soaking water has been absorbed and buckwheat softens like a thick porridge. Add milk and syrup to the final product and stir. Taste and adjust syrup and salt. Serve piping hot in breakfast bowls.

Preparation time: 30 minutes
Makes 2 servings

SOOTHING SOUPS AND STEWS

Lentil Wild Mushroom
Rainbow Root Vegetable
Split Pea
Creamless Cream of Cauliflower
Sweet Potato and Red Bean
Bold Black Bean
Summer Corn Chowder
White Bean and Rosemary

Lentil Wild Mushroom Soup

1 tablespoon unrefined extra virgin olive oil
1 small yellow onion, chopped
5 fresh garlic cloves, minced
2 medium carrots, chopped
1 cup shiitake mushrooms, thinly sliced
2 stalks celery, chopped
8 cups vegetable stock
2 cups dry lentils
Salt to taste
Freshly milled pepper
3 fresh or canned plum tomatoes, roughly cut
2 tablespoons wheat-free tamari

Heat large stock pot to medium high, then add olive oil. Add onion and cook over medium heat until it is translucent. As onion softens, add minced garlic. When onion is soft, add carrots and mushrooms. Cook for 2 minutes, until the colors begin to brighten. Add celery and stir for 1 minute.

Pour in stock and then add lentils. Bring soup to a boil, then lower heat to a simmer. Season with salt and pepper to taste. Cover and simmer for about 30 minutes or until lentils are tender. Add the tomatoes and tamari towards the end of cooking time and heat through.

Preparation time: 45 minutes
Makes 6 servings

Rainbow Root Vegetable Soup

Root vegetables are warming and sweet. This colorful stew-like soup will nourish you on a cold winter day.

2 tablespoons olive or canola oil
2 tablespoons fresh ginger, peeled and minced
5 cloves fresh garlic, minced
3/4 cup green onions, chopped
1 medium parsnip, peeled and cut into half moons
2 medium carrots, cut into discs
1 large rutabaga, peeled and cubed
2 medium purple potatoes, cubed
6 cups vegetable or chicken stock
Sea salt and crushed black pepper to taste
Cilantro for garnish

Heat stock pot to medium high, add olive oil. Sauté ginger and garlic for 1 minute. Add carrot, parsnip and rutabaga and sauté for about 3 minutes. Add vegetable or chicken stock and bring to a boil. Turn heat to low and simmer for 25 minutes or until vegetables are tender. Add sea salt and black pepper. Garnish with some chopped cilantro.

Preparation time: 40 minutes
Makes 4-5 servings

Split Pea Soup

2 cups split peas, washed several times and drained in a colander
6 cups spring water or vegetable stock
2 celery stalks, diced
2 carrots, diced
1 small onion, diced
1/8 cup wheat-free tamari
1 teaspoon dried basil
1 teaspoon dried marjoram
3 cloves fresh garlic, minced
3" piece kombu
Pinch of sea salt
Fresh lemon juice, to taste

Combine split peas, water and kombu in a soup pot and bring to a boil. Reduce heat to low and simmer for 45 minutes or until peas are soft. Stir frequently and add more water if necessary. While peas are cooking, steam vegetables, about 5 minutes. When peas are soft, add cooked vegetables and all seasonings, stir well. Simmer 10 minutes. Serve with a squeeze of lemon juice. Salt to taste.

Preparation time: 60 minutes
Makes 6 servings

Creamless Cream of Cauliflower Soup

1 head of cauliflower
2-6 tablespoons canola oil
1 large onion, chopped
4-8 cloves of garlic, minced
64-128 ounces of low sodium chicken or vegetable stock
1 cup white rice
Sea Salt (garlic salt or seasoned salt may be used) and pepper to taste

Heat large skillet to medium-high heat, then add canola oil. Sauté onion and 1-2 cloves of garlic until soft, about 5 minutes. Season with a dash of salt and pepper.

Wash and cut cauliflower into manageable florets. The stalk and leaves may be used if desired. Steam the cauliflower until tender in 2 cups of stock—about 10 minutes. Reserve the remaining stock.

When the onion and garlic are soft add rice and sauté in the onion until rice becomes opaque—about 5 minutes. 1-2 cloves of chopped garlic may be added. Season with a dash of salt and pepper.

When the rice is opaque add stock from the steamed cauliflower and two cans (16 ounces) of stock. Season with salt and pepper. Reduce heat and cover. Cook until rice is quite soft and beginning to fall apart. Do not allow the rice to absorb all the stock. Add more stock if necessary. **Note to whole foods purists:** using brown rice or other whole grains can add fiber and a small amount of nutrients to this dish but trials using these ingredients resulted in much greater cooking times, the use of much more stock and a porridge-like consistency and flavor that dominated the dish.

When the rice is fully cooked, add the cauliflower. 1-2 cloves of chopped garlic may be added. Season with a dash of salt and pepper. Add enough stock to cover cauliflower and simmer for at least 30 minutes uncovered.

Remove portions of the unpureed soup from the pan into a blender so not to overfill. Puree until velvety. Pour pureed soup into a new pan and heat on low temperature. Continue the process of pureeing until all the cauliflower is pureed with the rice base. Stir the pureed soup frequently.

Adjust seasoning with salt and pepper. Note that you are creating a large number of servings. Add salt incrementally, tasting for preference as you go.
Preparation time: 60 minutes
Makes 10 servings
Original recipe by Bret Rust, 2009

Sweet Potato and Red Bean Stew

3 teaspoons butter or 1 tablespoon unrefined extra virgin olive oil
1 medium red onion, diced
4 cloves fresh garlic, minced
4 medium sweet potatoes, cut into 1 inch cubes
1 large orange bell pepper, seeded and chopped
3 roma tomatoes, diced
2, 15 oz. cans aduki beans or kidney beans
6 cups vegetable broth or water
1/2 cup brown basmati rice
1/2 teaspoon curry powder
1/4 teaspoon cumin
Sea salt to taste

Heat medium-size stock pot to medium-high then add butter or oil. Sauté onion and garlic until onion becomes translucent. Add sweet potatoes and stir for 3 minutes. Add pepper and tomatoes, stir for 3 minutes. Add beans and stir for another minute. Add broth or water, rice, seasonings, cover pot and bring to a boil. Make sure liquid sits right above the level of vegetables. Reduce heat to low and simmer for about 30 minutes or until vegetables and rice are tender. Serve hot in bowls.

Preparation time: 50 minutes
Makes about 8 servings

Bold Black Bean Soup

2 tablespoons unrefined extra virgin olive oil
1 large white onion, diced
1 small red pepper, diced
3 cloves fresh garlic, minced
1 tablespoon cumin
1 tablespoon dried oregano
1 tablespoon chopped fresh thyme
3 canned chipotle peppers with sauce, chopped
8 cups chicken or vegetable stock
2 cups dry black beans (pre-soaked) or 2 cans black beans rinsed and strained
6 ounces coconut milk (1 small can)
Juice of 1 lime
Sea salt to taste

Garnish:
Chopped tomatoes
Dollop sour cream
Diced avocado
Fresh chopped cilantro
Sliced scallions

Heat olive oil over medium-high heat in a large stock pot. Add onion, red pepper and garlic, cooking until onions become translucent and start to brown, about 5 minutes. Add cumin, oregano, thyme, and chipotles, stir for 1 minute. Add 1 cup of stock first to deglaze the bottom of the pot. Follow by adding the rest of the stock and the black beans. Bring to a boil and then reduce heat to low and simmer, cover and let cook for about 1 1/2 hours, or until beans are soft.
Add coconut milk and lime juice and stir until evenly blended. Add salt to taste.
Garnish with a small dollop of sour cream in the center, topped with tomatoes, avocado, cilantro and scallions.

Preparation time: 2 hours
Makes 9 servings
Inspiration for this recipe came from Jared Rice, MS, RD, LDN

Summer Corn Chowder

5 cups water or stock
Kernels cut from 3 ears corn or 3 cups frozen corn
1 onion, diced
1 stock celery, diced
1/4 cup daikon radish (optional)
3" strip kombu seaweed
White or brown miso paste, to taste
Parsley

Simmer corn cobs and kombu in water for 10 minutes. Then remove cobs, add onion, celery & daikon. Simmer 10 minutes. Then remove cobs, add onion, celery, & daikon. Simmer 10 minutes, then add corn kernels and cook 10 more minutes. Dissolve miso into soup and remove kombu. For creamy texture, blend half in the blender. Reheat, and serve garnished with parsley.

Preparation time: 40 minutes
Makes 5 servings

White Bean and Rosemary Soup

2 cans white cannellini beans, strained and rinsed
1 tablespoon unrefined extra virgin olive oil
2 carrots, coarsely chopped
1 medium yellow onion, diced
2 large stalks celery, chopped
5 fresh garlic cloves, minced
2 sprigs rosemary
1 cup swiss chard leaves, sliced, with ribs removed
8 cups vegetable or chicken broth
2-3 tablespoons apple cider vinegar
Sea salt and crushed black pepper to taste
Variation: add 1/4 pound ground turkey or sausage and sauté with onions

Heat stock pot to medium high, then add olive oil. Sauté onions until they are translucent, about 3 minutes. Add celery, carrots, and rosemary and stir for 4 minutes. Add garlic, chard, beans, and broth. Increase heat to boiling, then reduce and simmer for 45 minutes. Add salt, pepper and cider vinegar to taste, removing rosemary before serving.

Preparation time: 60 minutes
Makes about 10 servings

VIVACIOUS VEGGIE SIDES

Cider Glazed Roasted Roots
Garlic Sautéed Collards
Shredded Daikon and Scallion Pancakes
Ginger Honey Carrots
Sake Braised Kale
Parsnip Sauté
Baked Delicata Squash
Hummus with Lime and Yogurt
Kidney Bean and Corn Salad with Cider Lime Vinaigrette
Rutabaga and Kale Sauté

Cider Glazed Roasted Root Vegetables

2 large carrots, peeled, cut into half moons, 1/2 inch thick
1 parsnip, peeled and cut into half moons, 1/2 inch thick
1 medium size rutabaga, peeled and cubed, 1/2 inch chunks
1 sweet potato, yellow or orange, cubed, 1/2 inch chunks
1 cup yellow onion, peeled and cubed, 1-inch chunks
2 tablespoons unrefined, extra virgin olive oil
1 1/2 tablespoons apple cider vinegar (raw if available)
2 tablespoons honey or agave nectar
1/2 teaspoon sea salt
1/4 teaspoon black pepper
Optional: 6 whole cloves of fresh garlic, peeled

Sea salt and crushed black pepper to taste

Preheat oven to 425 degrees.

Chop all vegetables and set aside in a large mixing bowl. In a small separate bowl, combine oil, vinegar, sweetener, salt and pepper and whisk together until mixture is smooth and thick. Pour liquid mixture over vegetables and toss until they are well coated. Grease a shallow baking dish or roasting pan with oil and spread vegetables out so they are densely packed on the pan.

Bake uncovered until tender, browned and caramelized, about 50-60 minutes. Stir vegetables occasionally during baking, about every 15 minutes, for even roasting. If more browning is needed at the end of cooking, increase heat to broil, and brown tops of vegetables for 2 minutes.

Preparation time: 1 hour and 15 minutes
Makes about 4 side dish servings

Garlic-Sautéed Collards

1 bunch collard greens, chopped
1 to 2 tablespoons extra-virgin olive oil
1 tablespoon garlic, minced
1 teaspoon brown rice vinegar
1/2 teaspoon tamari

Cut the leaves from the stem before washing. Wash greens carefully. Shake off excess water, pile leave on top of the other, and chop into squares.

Heat oil in a 10-inch skillet. Add garlic and sauté 1 minute. Make sure the heat is low enough that the garlic doesn't burn.

Add greens and keep them moving in the skillet. Turn frequently so that all greens reach the heat. When the greens turn bright green and begin to wilt, remove from heat. Toss with vinegar and tamari and serve warm.

Preparation time: 15 minutes
Makes 4 servings

Shredded Daikon and Scallion Pancakes with Cilantro and Sour Cream

Daikon is a long white Japanese radish, often served raw or pickled, in a salad or as a condiment. Serve up these Asian-style latkes as an appetizer or side dish, anytime of the day.

1 medium daikon radish, about 1 1/2 cups grated
2 green onions, chopped
1 clove fresh garlic, minced
1 medium egg, beaten
3 tablespoons gluten-free flour (rice, sorghum or a blend)
1/2 teaspoon sea salt
1/8 teaspoon crushed black pepper
Unrefined extra virgin olive oil for frying

For Garnish:
1/4 cup sour cream
1/4 cup fresh cilantro, chopped coarsely

Shred daikon with a grater into a sieve, strainer or colander. Set aside over a bowl to allow excess water drain from daikon for about 8 minutes.

Combine shredded daikon with green onions and garlic. Add egg. Sprinkle flour, salt and pepper and stir.

Heat skillet to medium high, add olive oil. Drop mixture by tablespoons into pan, pancakes should be about 2 x 2 inches. Brown on both sides, approximately 5 minutes for each side.

Top off with a dollop of sour cream and garnish with cilantro.
Variation: blend sour cream, cilantro and 1 clove of garlic in a food processor and serve as garnish.

Preparation time: 15 minutes
Makes 8-10 pancakes

Ginger Honey Carrots

2 large carrots, peeled and cut into half moons
1 tablespoon honey
1 tablespoon unrefined extra virgin olive oil
Pinch sea salt
Pinch black pepper
1 tablespoon fresh ginger, peeled and minced

Coat carrots with honey, 1 tablespoon of olive oil, salt and pepper. Heat sauté pan to medium high, then add the remaining olive oil. Sauté minced ginger in pan until it turns light brown and starts to crackle. Add carrots and sauté until soft, approximately 10 minutes.

Preparation time: 15 minutes
Makes 1-2 servings

Sake-Braised Kale

2 tablespoons unrefined extra virgin olive oil
6 cups fresh kale leaves
2 teaspoons fresh ginger, peeled and minced
2 cloves fresh garlic, minced
1/4 cup cooking sake or mirin (Japanese rice wine)
Sea salt to taste

Wash kale thoroughly and de-stem leaves. Heat sauté pan to medium high, then add olive oil. Sauté kale until it reduces in size by one-half. Add ginger and garlic, stir for 1 minute. Add cooking sake and reduce heat to low. Let kale simmer for about 2 minutes, then serve.

Preparation time: 15 minutes
Makes 2 servings

Parsnip Sauté

1 large parsnip, peeled, cut into half moons, 1/8 inch thick
1 tablespoon agave nectar
1 tablespoon rice vinegar
2 tablespoons mirin (optional)
1/2 teaspoon sea salt
1/8 teaspoon black pepper
1 tablespoon unrefined extra virgin olive oil
1/2 cup white or yellow onion, chopped
2 tablespoons green onion, chopped

Coat parsnip with agave, rice vinegar, mirin, salt and pepper. Let sit for 5 minutes. Heat sauté pan to medium high, then add olive oil. Saute onion until it becomes translucent. Add parsnip and sauté until golden brown and soft. Garnish with green onion.

Preparation time: 15 minutes
Makes 2 servings

Baked Delicata Squash

1 tablespoon unrefined extra virgin olive oil
2 teaspoons wheat-free tamari
1 tablespoons maple syrup, honey or agave nectar
1/2 teaspoon sea salt
1/8 teaspoon crushed black pepper
1 delicata squash, halved and de-seeded
2 tablespoons cilantro, chopped

Preheat oven to 400 degrees.

Combine oil, tamari, syrup, salt and pepper in small bowl. Whisk together and set aside. Cut squash in half, scrape out the seeds with a spoon. Do not peel the skin off. Brush liquid mixture over squash flesh.

Place squash face down on a shallow baking dish. Bake for approximately 20 minutes or until soft. Garnish with cilantro.

Preparation time: 25 minutes
Makes 2 servings

Hummus with Lime and Yogurt

Garbanzos or chick peas are a staple food in the Mediterranean diet. These beans are nutrient powerhouses, high in protein, folate and essential fatty acids. This recipe transcends the standard olive oil, lemon, and tahini hummus. Yogurt gives it a creamy texture and lime infuses acidity and balance. Serve morning, noon or night with your favorite chips or dipping veggies.

1 can no salt garbanzo beans, drained and rinsed
2-3 tablespoons high quality unrefined extra virgin olive oil
juice of half of a lime
1 tablespoon plain yogurt (whole milk is preferred)
1 tablespoon sesame tahini
splash of balsamic vinegar
1/8 teaspoon crushed black pepper
1/2 teaspoon sea salt
1/8 teaspoon fresh garlic, minced (garlic powder will do if fresh is unavailable)
1-2 tablespoons water

Combine all ingredients except for the water in a food processor. After all ingredients are combined, add 1 tablespoon of water, pulse again. If consistency of hummus is too thick add another tablespoon of water.

Prep time: 5-10 minutes
Makes: 2-3 servings

Kidney Bean and Corn Salad with Cider Lime Vinaigrette

Kidney beans and fresh corn have a sweet flavor and are good sources of protein. Paired with a cooling cider lime vinaigrette, this salsa inspired salad is great on a hot summer day.

2 cups kidney beans, cooked (canned beans, drained and rinsed, can be used if pressure cooker is not available)
3 ears of fresh corn, approximately 1 1/2 cups
3/4 cup fresh red pepper, diced
1/2 cup red onion, diced
2 sprigs fresh cilantro
2 cloves fresh garlic, minced

Soak kidney beans overnight. Pressure cook beans for approximately 20-40 minutes in 6 cups of water. Drain beans and let cool until room temperature.

Remove husks from corn. Bring water in a pot to boil. Place corn in boiling water. Turn off heat. Remove corn after 4 minutes, let stand until corn returns to room temperature. Remove kernels from corn cob using chef's knife. Combine cooked beans, corn kernels, red pepper, red onion, garlic and cilantro in large mixing bowl.
Prep time: 15-20 minutes
Serves: 4-6

For the Vinaigrette
4 tablespoons raw apple cider vinegar
2 tablespoons unrefined extra virgin olive oil
1 tablespoon light brown sugar
1 tablespoon fresh lime juice
1/2 teaspoon sea salt
1/4 teaspoon black pepper
Combine all ingredients in a mixing bowl. Whisk together until mixture thickens slightly. Pour over kidney bean salad until all ingredients are well coated.
Prep time: 5 minutes
Serves: 4-6

Rutabaga and Kale Sauté

Rutabagas are sweet, starchy root vegetables. They are the sibling of the turnip although they have yellow flesh. When you visit the grocery, it's hard to discern between them, they're almost twin siblings. Their sweetness is their most appealing attribute. They're not quite as sweet as a yam but are definitely sweeter than your average white potato. They are perfect in the wintertime, like most root vegetables, roasted, sautéed, stewed and in soups. Kids love them too. Rutabaga pairs deliciously with kale. Try this quick and easy sauté for a nutrient dense side dish that you can serve with chicken, fish, rice and other grains.

1 tablespoon unrefined extra-virgin olive oil
3 green onions, chopped
1/8 teaspoon sea salt
1 large rutabaga, chopped into thin rectangular pieces, 1/8 inch thick
1 1/2 cups kale, chopped
3 tablespoons cooking sake or mirin (Japanese rice wine)
Optional: 1 tablespoon wheat-free tamari

Peel the skin off rutabaga with a carrot peeler and chop into thin rectangular pieces (1/8 inch thick) to accelerate cooking time.

Bring saucepan to medium heat, then add olive oil. Sauté 3/4 of green onions (save some for garnish) until soft and glistening. Add rutabaga and saute until brown and soft. Combine kale with rutabaga and add cooking sake. After vegetables absorb sake, reduce heat to low and remove from heat. Serve warm, with a splash of tamari and garnish with green onions.

Preparation time: 10-15 minutes
Makes 1-2 servings

GLORIOUS GRAINS

Confetti Quinoa with Nori, Sesame and Cashew
Toasted Buckwheat with Squash and Yams
Millet Salad with Fennel and Cannelini Beans
Ginger Shiitake Rice
Quinoa Biryani
Cheesy Polenta Squares
Herbed Rice Pilaf

Confetti Quinoa with Nori, Sesame and Raw Cashews

1 cup quinoa, dry
2 cups water
1 tablespoon unrefined extra-virgin olive oil
2 cloves garlic, minced
1 teaspoon ginger, minced
3/4 cup celery and leaves, chopped
2-3 tablespoons toasted sesame oil
2 tablespoons wheat-free tamari
1/2 cup dried nori (about 2 toasted nori sheets, Eden-brand), crushed or torn
2 teaspoons sesame seeds
1/4 cup raw cashews, crushed
Sea salt and crushed black pepper to taste
Optional: 1/2 cup beans (aduki, black or white beans)

Combine water and quinoa in covered pot. After water comes to a boil, turn heat to low and simmer for about 15 minutes or until all of the water has been absorbed. Fluff with a fork and cool.

Heat saucepan to medium-high heat, then add olive oil. Sauté garlic and ginger about 1 minute. Turn heat to medium, add quinoa and sauté for 1 minute. Add celery, sesame oil and tamari and mix until quinoa is coated. Crumple nori sheets as you would a piece of paper, sprinkle over mixture. Top with cashews and sesame seeds and mix again.

Preparation time: 25 minutes
Makes 2-3 servings

Toasted Buckwheat with Squash and Yams

A misnomer, buckwheat is not part of the wheat family. It is a seed of a weed-like plant related to rhubarb, not a grain. Buckwheat cooks up very quickly. This dish is perfect in the fall or winter months, loaded with vitamins A and C and bioactive compounds from mushrooms. Eat your groats!

1 cup delicata squash, chopped, with skin, no seeds
1 cup yam, chopped, with skin
1 tablespoon unrefined extra virgin olive oil

1 cup whole buckwheat groats
2 cups boiling water (can substitute vegetable or chicken stock for water)
1/2 teaspoon sea salt

1 bunch kale
1 tablespoon olive oil
5 cloves of garlic, minced
1 cup shiitake or crimini mushrooms, chopped
Sea salt to taste

Preheat oven to 350° F. Combine squash and yam with olive oil and place in roasting pan. Roast in preheated oven until tender, stirring occasionally.

While squash and yam are roasting, toast groats in a dry pan over medium heat until it separates, dries, and gives off a toasty aroma, about 3 minutes. Pour boiling water over the groats and stir. Stir in the salt. Cover. Reduce heat to low and cook for 15 minutes. Tilt pan slightly to see if any water has not been incorporated. If so, continue cooking until no water remains. Fluff with fork.

While the groats are cooking, prepare mushroom kale mixture. Remove kale stems chop the leaves finely. Set aside. Heat a skillet to medium heat and add olive oil. Sauté garlic for 1 minute and add mushrooms. Sauté 1 minute and add kale leaves. Sauté until garlic is just beginning to turn golden and kale leaves are tender.

Assemble dish by combining groats, squash and yam, and mushroom kale mixture. Careful to not overmix or groats will turn mushy. Salt to taste.

Preparation time: 25 minutes
Makes 4-6 servings

Millet Salad with Fennel and Cannelini Beans

1 cup millet, dry and toasted
2 1/4 cups water
Pinch of sea salt
1 15 oz. can cannelini beans, drained and rinsed
2 green onions, chopped
2 cloves fresh garlic, minced
1 tablespoon rice vinegar
2 tablespoons walnut oil or extra virgin olive oil
1 small fennel bulb, cut in half and cored
Juice of 1/4 of a lemon
1 tablespoon chopped fennel leaves
1 tablespoon chopped parsley
1 tablespoon high quality extra virgin olive oil
1/2 cup walnuts, chopped

Heat a dry pot to medium. Add millet. Stir grain with a wooden spoon. After a few minutes the grains will begin to pop and give off a nutty aroma. Add water and salt. Bring to a boil then reduce heat to low and simmer, covered, for approximately 20-30 minutes, stirring occasionally. When all of the water has been absorbed, remove from heat. Fluff with a fork and allow to cool slightly.

In a mixing bowl combine beans, onions, garlic, salt, vinegar, 2 tablespoons of oil and mix well. Slice fennel very thin and spritz with lemon juice to prevent discoloration. Add to bean mixture along with fennel leaves and parsley. Stir gently to combine and adjust seasoning if needed. Add beans and seasonings to millet and stir well. Add remaining 1 tablespoon of olive oil to the final product, sprinkle with walnuts and serve.

Preparation time: 40 minutes
Makes 4 servings

Recipe adapted by Genevieve Sherrow, MS, CN with inspiration from Mary Shaw

Ginger Shiitake Rice

1 cup long grain white rice
2 cups water
1/2 teaspoon sea salt
2 tablespoons toasted sesame oil
8 ounces fresh shiitake mushrooms, stems removed, caps sliced
1 large red or yellow bell pepper, thinly sliced
2 teaspoons fresh ginger, peeled and minced
2 green onions, chopped
3 tablespoons wheat-free tamari
Crushed black pepper to taste

Combine rice, water and salt in medium saucepan, bring to boil over high heat. Mix in rice. Reduce heat to low, cover and cook until rice is tender and water is absorbed, about 20 minutes. Remove from heat and let stand for 5 minutes.

Heat sesame oil in skillet over medium-high heat. Add mushrooms; Sauté 2 minutes. Add pepper and ginger; Sauté 3 minutes. Add rice, onions and soy sauce and toss. Taste and adjust salt and pepper.

Preparation time: 35 minutes
Makes about 2-3 servings

Adapted by Genevieve Sherrow from *Gourmet Magazine*

Quinoa Biryani

1 cup quinoa, rinsed
2 cups vegetable or chicken stock
Pinch of sea salt
2 tablespoons unrefined coconut oil
1 tablespoon ginger, peeled and minced
1 1/2 cups sweet onion, diced
3 cloves garlic, crushed
3/4 cup golden raisins
1/2 cup raw almonds, crushed
1/2 teaspoon turmeric
1-2 tablespoons honey
1/8 teaspoon cinnamon
1/8 teaspoon coriander
Sea salt and crushed black pepper to taste

Combine stock, quinoa and pinch of sea salt in covered pot. After water comes to a boil, turn heat to low and simmer for about 15 minutes or until all of the water has been absorbed. Remove from heat, fluff with a fork and cool. Do not stir or agitate quinoa during cooking. Tilt pot to 45 degree angle to see if water has been absorbed. Remove quinoa from heat and let it cool completely, about 10 minutes.

While quinoa is cooking, heat saucepan to medium-high, then add coconut oil. Sauté ginger until it sizzles. Add onion and stir until it's translucent. Add garlic, turmeric, cinnamon, coriander and stir.

Combine cooled quinoa, raisins, almonds, and honey (in that order) with garlic and onion mixture. Stir until ingredients are well-coated. Sea salt and black pepper to taste.

Preparation time: 35 minutes
Makes 3-4 servings

Cheesy Polenta Triangles

This is a nice adaptation to traditional polenta. The chile pepper flakes add a nice kick to this otherwise mild dish. Serve with a bean salad or a fresh summer salsa.

2 cups vegetable or chicken stock
3 cups water
pinch of sea salt
1-2 teaspoons red chile pepper flakes
3 tablespoons unrefined extra virgin olive oil
1 cup polenta
1/4 cup sharp provolone

Add water and stock to a 2-quart pot and bring to a boil. Add salt, red chile pepper flakes and 1 tablespoon olive oil. Slowly add polenta while stirring steadily with whisk.
Reduce heat to low and continue stirring, using a wooden spoon, for 30-40 minutes. Adjust heat to maintain a slight puckering of the polenta. Polenta grains should appear creamy. Use additional water to achieve this consistency.

Once creamy, remove polenta from heat and stir in cheese. Use 1 tablespoon to lightly oil a 9 1/2 x 13 1/2 baking dish or two 8x8 baking dishes. Pour polenta in the baking dish and place in the refrigerator for 30-45 minutes or until cool. Once polenta is cool, slice into triangles.

Heat a large cast iron skillet with olive oil. Pan is hot enough if you place a slice of polenta on it and it lightly sizzles. Fry polenta slices until slightly golden brown, then flip. Once both sides are fried, place slices on a plate with a paper towel to absorb any extra oil. Serve with *Kidney Bean and Corn Salad.*

Preparation time: 1 1/2 - 2 hours (includes cooling time)
Makes 4-6 servings

Herbed Rice Pilaf

4 1/2 cups water
1 cup brown rice
1 cup wild rice
1 1/2 cups mushrooms, sliced
1 teaspoon wheat-free tamari
1 medium onion, coarsely chopped
2 garlic cloves, minced
1/2 teaspoon sage
1/2 teaspoon cumin
1/2 teaspoon thyme

Combine all ingredients in saucepan. Stir well and bring pot to boil. Reduce heat to low and simmer for about 45 minutes or until rice is tender and all of the water has been absorbed.

Preparation time: 50 minutes
Makes 8-10 servings

MAIN DISHES

Coconut Curry Chicken with Plum Wine
Thai Style Bouillabaisse
Aduki Bean Rice Tacos
Millet Lentil Croquettes with Watercress Pesto
Mediterranean Stuffed Peppers
Nori-dusted Pan-Fried Flounder
Tuscan Beans and Greens
Eat the Rainbow Veggie Chili
Chickpea Vegetable Curry
Habana Rice and Beans

Coconut Curry Chicken with Plum Wine

1 tablespoon extra virgin unrefined olive oil or canola oil
4-5 organic, pastured chicken thighs
1 can whole coconut milk
3/4 cup plain rice milk
3 teaspoons green curry paste
1 tablespoon raw honey or agave nectar
1/4 cup plum wine (can substitute cooking sake or mirin)
1/2 tablespoon fish sauce
1 cup cilantro, coarsely chopped
Lime to taste

Heat sauté pan to medium-high, then add olive oil. Brown chicken thighs on both sides, about 5 minutes per side. Add coconut milk, rice milk, curry paste and stir. Next, add honey and plum wine. Cover pot, turn heat to low and let chicken simmer for 20 minutes. Top off with fish sauce before serving. Garnish with cilantro and a squeeze of lime.

Preparation time: 40 minutes
Makes 4-5 servings

Thai Style Bouillabaisse

2 tablespoons unrefined extra virgin olive oil, for frying
1 small red onion (about 3/4 cup), chopped
4 cloves fresh garlic, minced
4 red bliss or Yukon gold potatoes, cubed 1/2 inch pieces
1 large zucchini, halved and cut diagonally or slanted
1 1/2 cups red cabbage, shredded
2 cups lacinato kale, chopped
1 small red pepper (about 1 cup), chopped
7 pinches of sea salt
1/2 cup basil, chopped
1 can coconut milk
1/2 cup whole milk or rice milk
2 tablespoons fish sauce
1 tablespoon wheat-free tamari
Sea salt and crushed black pepper to taste
1/2 pound of smoked salmon or smoked black cod
Basil leaves for garnish

Heat a medium-size stock pot to medium high, then add 1 tablespoon of oil. Sauté onion, garlic and 1 pinch salt until onion becomes translucent. Add potatoes and 3 pinches of salt, sauté for 4 minutes. Add zucchini and 1 pinch of salt, sauté for 3 minutes. Add 1 tablespoon of olive oil, cabbage, kale, red pepper, 3 pinches of salt and stir thoroughly for 3 minutes. Add basil, milks, fish sauce, tamari and bring to a boil. Immediately reduce heat and simmer stew for approximately 15-20 minutes or until potatoes are soft. Do not overcook.

Serve in bowls and top off with some basil leaves and smoked salmon.

Preparation time: 50 minutes
Makes about 5 servings, 1 cup each

Aduki Bean Rice Tacos

Aduki beans, otherwise known as adzuki or azuki beans, are cultivated throughout East Asian countries. They are loaded with iron, B vitamins, protein, magnesium and potassium. Their low glycemic index makes them an optimal choice for people with blood sugar management issues. In Traditional Chinese Medicine, aduki beans are well known for their strengthening qualities and "yang" energy. Adukis pair well with grains and vegetables in savory dishes. Try incorporating them into your cooking with this Asian and Mexican inspired dish.

1 can Eden brand aduki beans, drained and rinsed
1 cup brown basmati rice
2 cups water
3/4 teaspoon sea salt
1 tablespoon toasted sesame oil
2 tablespoons fresh ginger, peeled and minced
2 teaspoons umeboshi plum vinegar
1 teaspoon red chili flakes
1/4 cup green onions, chopped
1/4 cup cilantro, chopped
1/2 cup sprouted almonds or raw cashews, chopped
8 soft corn tortillas

Bring rice and 2 cups of water to a boil in medium saucepan, and add 1/4 teaspoon salt. Reduce heat to low and simmer, covered, for about 25 minutes, or until water is absorbed and grains are dry. Remove from heat, and let stand 5 minutes.

Heat ginger and sesame oil in medium skillet over medium heat until ginger begins to sizzle, about 3 minutes. Add beans, vinegar, chili flakes, nuts and remaining 1/2 teaspoon salt. Cook over medium-high heat, stirring often, about 3 minutes, or until liquid evaporates.

Stir rice into bean mixture. Taste, and add more salt if desired. Sprinkle with chopped green onions and cilantro. Serve on warm corn tortillas.

Preparation time: 30 minutes
Makes: 8 servings

Recipe adapted by Genevieve Sherrow from the *Vegetarian Times*

Millet Lentil Croquettes with Watercress Pesto

This is a great way to use leftover beans and grains. Use this template to make endless croquette combinations. The pesto can be used as a dipping sauce or in the croquettes themselves for added flavor and color.

For the Croquettes:
1/2 cup millet, soaked overnight in 1 1/2 cups water and cooked
1/2 cup red lentils (dry), cooked
2 medium sunchokes
2 medium carrots
2 celery stalks
1/2 yellow onion
6 cloves garlic
1 tablespoon coconut oil plus coconut oil for frying
1 teaspoon salt
1/2 teaspoon black pepper
1 teaspoon cumin
pinch of cayenne pepper
1 tablespoon lemon juice
1/2 cup cilantro, chopped
2 eggs

Prepare the millet and lentils and place in large bowl. Place the sunchokes, carrots, celery, onion and garlic in a food processor and pulse until the vegetables are diced. Add salt, pepper, cumin and cayenne and sauté the vegetables in coconut oil for 7 minutes, until the mixture is aromatic and the onions are translucent. Mix the vegetables with the millet and lentils. Add lemon juice, cilantro, eggs and mix well. Take half of the mixture and food process until smooth. Return to the bowl. Form 8-10 croquettes and fry in coconut oil, about 10 minutes on each side.

For the Pesto:
1 clove garlic
1 cup pumpkin seeds, toasted
1 cup watercress
1 cup cilantro
2 tablespoons lemon juice
3 tablespoons olive oil
½ teaspoon cumin
½ teaspoon salt

Place the garlic and pumpkin seeds in the food processor and puree into a fine paste. Add the remaining ingredients and puree until desired consistency is reached. Place a spoonful of the pesto on top of each croquette.

Preparation time: 1 hour
Makes 4-6 servings

Original Recipe by Ryah Nabielski, 2009.

Mediterranean Stuffed Peppers

Stuffed peppers are a show-stopping, tried-and-true dinner classic. In this version, pomegranate juice and dried figs give it a Mediterranean feel.

4 large yellow or red bell peppers
3/4 cup pomegranate or cranberry juice
1/2 cup dried figs, stemmed and chopped
1 1/2 cups cooked wild rice
1 cup diced yellow squash
1/2 cup feta cheese, crumbled
1/2 cup chopped walnuts

Preheat oven to 400 degrees F.

Cut tops off peppers to use as lids. Scrape out seeds and ribs with knife. Combine pomegranate juice and figs in large saucepan, and cook over medium heat 7 to 10 minutes, or until figs soften and juice reduces and becomes syrupy. Remove from heat, and stir in rice, squash, feta cheese and walnuts. Fill peppers with mixture, and set in 9x13-inch baking pan. Place tops on peppers. Add ½ inch water to pan, and cover with foil.
Bake 30 to 40 minutes, or until peppers are tender with slightly wrinkled skins and filling is hot.

Preparation time: 25 minutes to pressure-cook rice and 40-50 minutes for remaining preparation and baking.

Makes 4 servings

Adapted from *Vegetarian Times* Magazine

Nori-Dusted Pan-Fried Flounder

1 pound fresh flounder fillet**
1 tablespoon ume plum vinegar
juice of 1 small lime
1/2 teaspoon sea salt
1/4 teaspoon crushed black pepper
dash of garlic powder
2 tablespoons unrefined, extra virgin olive oil
1 toasted sushi nori sheet (Eden-brand), crushed and torn
1/4 cup cilantro, chopped coarsely (for garnish)
2 roma tomatoes, cut into quarters

***Variation:* Halibut, cod, tilapia or rockfish fish fillet can be substituted for the flounder

Wash fish under cold water and pat dry with paper towel. In a small bowl, combine vinegar, lime, salt, pepper and garlic. Heat skillet to medium-high then add olive oil. Brown fish on both sides. *Note:* fish cooks 10 minutes per inch of thickness regardless of type of fish or cooking technique. Do not over cook. Crumple and tear nori sheets into confetti size pieces. Sprinkle on top of fish with cilantro. Serve with tomatoes.

Preparation time: 10 minutes
Makes 2 servings

Tuscan Beans and Greens

1 tablespoon unrefined extra virgin olive oil
1/8 teaspoon crushed red pepper
2 garlic cloves, minced
1/4 cup dry white wine
1 cup vegetable or chicken broth
1 cups cannellini beans or other white beans, cooked
2 cups swiss chard, chopped
2 tablespoons fresh basil, chopped
Sea salt and crushed black pepper to taste

Heat olive oil in a large skillet over medium-high heat. Add pepper and garlic to pan, cook 20 seconds, stirring constantly. Stir in wine; cook 1 minute or until most of liquid evaporates. Stir in broth and beans; cook 2 minutes. Add swiss chard; cook until wilted. Remove from heat, stir in basil. Season with salt and pepper.

Preparation time: 20 minutes
Makes 4 servings, 3/4 cup each

Adapted from *Cooking Light Magazine*

Eat the Rainbow Veggie Chili

You've heard about "Eating the Rainbow". Now you can do it in one meal with this colorful, salsa-inspired chili. It's a satisfying lunch or dinner. Serve it with corn chips or corn tortillas if you're gluten-free. Splash it with lime before it goes into your mouth.

1 can black beans, rinsed
1 can kidney beans, rinsed
2 tablespoons high quality extra virgin olive oil
1 small yellow onion, diced
5 cloves fresh garlic, minced
2 small or 1 medium zucchini, halved and cut into half moons
1 small red pepper, diced
1 medium carrot, diced
1 cup chunky salsa
1/2 cup water
3/4 cup frozen corn (fresh if in season)
4 pinches of sea salt
Optional:
4 lime wedges
Corn chips or corn tortillas

Open cans and empty beans into a strainer, rinse thoroughly. Heat a stock pot to medium-high, then add olive oil. Add onion, garlic and 1 pinch of salt and saute until onion becomes translucent. Reduce heat to medium and add zucchini and 1 pinch of salt, stir for 2 minutes. Add beans and stir. Add red pepper, carrot, salsa, water, corn and remaining salt and stir until all ingredients are integrated.

Reduce heat to low and let simmer for about 10 minutes. Taste and adjust salt as needed. Serve with a squeeze of lime.

Preparation time: about 25 minutes
Makes 3-4 servings

Chickpea Vegetable Curry

Serve this curry dish with *Garlic Sautéed Collards* and a side of rice or quinoa for a vegan meal with Eastern flavors.

1 tablespoon unrefined extra virgin olive oil
1 cup yellow onion (about 1/2 of an onion), chopped
1 tablespoon curry powder
1 teaspoon sea salt
3 cloves of garlic, minced
1 large carrot, sliced
1 15 oz. can diced tomatoes
1 15 oz. can chickpeas, drained and rinsed
2 cups kale or spinach chopped
Cayenne pepper to taste

Heat olive oil in a medium skillet or pot over medium heat. Add the sliced onion, curry powder, salt and garlic (begin with 1/2 teaspoon each of salt and curry, adjust seasonings after the remaining ingredients are incorporated). Sauté, stirring often, until onion begins to soften, about 5 minutes.

Add the chickpeas and tomatoes. Simmer until hot, about 10 minutes. Add the kale or spinach towards the end of cooking to avoid overcooking.

Preparation time: 15 minutes
Makes 3 servings

Habana Rice and Beans

Rice:
2 tablespoons high quality unrefined extra virgin olive oil
1 1/4 cups yellow onion, chopped
4 cloves fresh garlic, minced
1 cup celery, chopped
1 tablespoon jalapeno pepper, seeded and minced
1/8 teaspoon sea salt
1 1/2 cups basmati rice, dry
3 1/2 cups water
1 15 oz. can of black, adzuki or kidney beans, drained and rinsed in a colander

Remaining ingredients:
1 cup red or yellow bell pepper, chopped
1/2 teaspoon black pepper
1 teaspoon ground cumin
1 teaspoon ground coriander
1/2 teaspoon sea salt
2 cups diced pineapple
1/4 cup minced fresh cilantro
Sea salt to taste
Chopped cilantro for garnish

Heat a large nonstick skillet to medium-high heat until hot, then add olive oil. Add onion, garlic, 1/8 teaspoon of salt and sauté until onion becomes translucent, about 3 minutes. Add celery and jalapeno and stir for 2 minutes. Add rice, cook 1 minute. Add 3 1/2 cups water; bring to a boil. Cover, reduce heat to low, and simmer 20 minutes. Add beans; cover, and simmer 10 minutes, stirring occasionally.

Stir in bell pepper, black pepper, cumin, and coriander, and cook 5 minutes. Stir in pineapple and cilantro; cook 2 minutes.

Serve hot and garnish with chopped cilantro.

Preparation time: 50 minutes
Makes 6 servings

Sweet Things

Maple Baked Apples

4 apples, cored
1/2 cup almond, pecans or raw cashews, crushed
1/4 teaspoon ground cinnamon
2 teaspoons maple syrup
1/4 teaspoon ground ginger
1 cup white grape juice

Preheat oven to 350 degrees. In a small bowl, mix together nuts, cinnamon, syrup and ginger. Place about 2 tablespoons of mixture into the core of each apple. Place apples in 9"x 9" baking pan. Pour white grape juice around apples. Bake until apples are cooked thoroughly and soft, about 40 minutes.

Preparation time: 50 minutes
Makes 4 servings

Apricot-Glazed Pears

This delectable dessert delivers high calorie density in an intensely flavorful preparation. Add a puree of seasonal berries or a creamy caramel sauce to enhance the presentation and boost the flavor quotient.

2 cups orange juice
4 small pears, halved, peeled, and cored
1/3 cup apricot jam
1 cup whipped cream

Bring orange juice to a boil in a medium saucepan. Add pears and simmer for 15 minutes or until pears are tender when pierced with a fork. Remove pears and place on paper towels to remove excess liquid.

Continue to boil orange juice until reduced by half.

Combine jam and ¼ cup of the reduced orange juice. Place pears in a 2-quart rectangular baking dish, cut side down; spoon sauce over top. Bake in a 350 degree oven for about 25 minutes or until pears are tender.

Serve warm pears in individual dessert dishes. Spoon sauce over pears. If desired, serve with ¼ cup whipped cream.

Preparation time: 60 minutes
Makes 4 servings.

Perfect Pumpkin Bread

1 1/4 cups white rice flour
3/4 cup Bob's Red Mill Gluten-free Flour Blend
1/2 teaspoon salt
1/2 teaspoon baking soda
1/2 teaspoon baking powder
1 teaspoon ground cinnamon
1/4 teaspoon cloves
1/2 teaspoon nutmeg
1 15 oz. can pumpkin puree
1 cup brown sugar, packed
2 eggs, beaten
1/3 cup coconut milk
2 tablespoons coconut or canola oil
1/2 cup pecans, chopped
3/4 cup golden raisins, currants or chopped dates

Preheat oven to 350 degrees F. Combine dry ingredients in large mixing bowl and whisk together until all ingredients are incorporated. With a hand mixer, beat eggs, pumpkin, sugar, milk and oil in a separate bowl until mixture is smooth. Slowly add dry ingredients to wet ingredients, beat together on low speed until mixture is smooth, without lumps. Fold in dried fruit and nuts with a wooden spoon.

Lightly grease a loaf pan with butter or oil. Pour batter into loaf pan. Bake bread at 350 degrees for about 60 minutes. Test for doneness with a wooden toothpick in the center of the loaf. If toothpick emerges clean, then bread is done.

Cool on a wire rack for about 15 minutes. Then remove from pan and continue cooling.

Prep time: 1 hour 10 minutes
Makes 7 servings

Cinnamon Peach Crisp

1 cup certified gluten-free oats
1/4 cup gluten-free flour blend
1/8 teaspoon sea salt
1/4 cup canola or safflower oil
3 tablespoons maple syrup
1/3 cup walnuts or pecans, chopped
3 peaches (about 5-6 cups), white or yellow flesh, sliced
1 teaspoon cinnamon
2 tablespoons brown sugar
Variation: apples can be used when peaches are not in season

Preheat oven to 350 degrees F. Mix oats, flour and salt in a bowl. Add oil and syrup; mix well. Stir in nuts and set aside. In a small bowl, combine peaches cinnamon and brown sugar.

Place fruit in lightly oiled 8" X 8" baking dish. Spoon the oat-nut mixture evenly over the top of the fruit. Cover and bake 30 minutes or until fruit is soft and sizzling. Uncover and bake 10 minutes more until the topping browns.

Preparation time: 60 minutes (15 minutes to prepare, 40 minutes to cook)
Makes 6 servings

Banana Walnut Bread

1 cup brown rice flour
1 cup white rice flour
1/4 cup each potato starch flour and tapioca flour
1 teaspoon xanthan gum
1 tablespoon gluten free baking powder
1/2 teaspoon salt
1/2 cup walnuts, chopped
1 egg
1/2 cup butter, melted
2/3 cups brown sugar
1-1/2 cups thoroughly mashed overripe bananas

Mix bananas with butter and sugar. Oil one standard or two small loaf pans, (or six mini-loafs). Stir dry ingredients into wet ingredients until moist. Immediately put the batter in the pans and bake at 350 degrees for 40 minutes to an hour depending on loaf size. Cool on rack.

Preparation time: 60 minutes
Makes 6-7 servings

Baked Bosc Pears a la Glace

4 medium firm to ripe Bosc pears, halved
1/4 cup maple syrup
Cinnamon
Vanilla ice cream

Preheat the oven to 350 F. Wash pears, halve lengthwise, and remove cores and stem ends. Drizzle syrup over the pears, and sprinkle with a little cinnamon. Place flesh side down in a 9 by 9-inch nonstick baking pan. Shift the pears around slightly about 15 minutes into the baking time. Bake until the pears are tender but not overcooked, about 20 minutes. Serve warm in shallow dishes over vanilla ice cream.

Preparation time: 25 minutes
Makes 4 servings

Pumpkin Corn Muffins

1 cup yellow cornmeal (I use Arrowhead Mills GF Corn Meal)
1/2 cup Bob's Red Mill GF Flour Blend
1/2 cup sorghum flour
1 teaspoon ground cinnamon
1/2 teaspoon pumpkin pie spice
1/2 teaspoon salt
1 1/2 teaspoons baking soda
2 eggs
1 15 oz. can pumpkin puree
1 cup light brown sugar, packed
1/4 cup milk

Preheat oven to 350 degrees.

Combine cornmeal, flours, cinnamon, spice, salt, soda in medium size bowl and whisk together until all ingredients are incorporated, set aside. In a separate bowl, whisk together eggs, pumpkin, sugar and milk. Pour dry ingredients in thirds into bowl with wet ingredients. With a hand mixer, mix thoroughly, until mixture is smooth, without lumps.

Spoon mixture into greased muffin tins. Bake for approximately 20-30 minutes. Check for doneness in the middle of muffins with a wooden toothpick. If toothpick emerges clean, muffins are done.

Remove muffins from tray. Cool on wire racks for about 10 minutes before serving.

Makes 12 medium size muffins
Preparation time: 50 minutes

The Warrior's Jewish Apple Cake

1 cup sweet sorghum flour
1/2 cup Bob's Red Mill GF Flour Blend
1/2 cup white rice flour
1 1/4 teaspoons baking soda
1/4 teaspoon sea salt
1 teaspoon cinnamon
1 1/4 cups brown sugar, packed
3 eggs
6 oz. whole milk, full fat plain yogurt
2 small apples about 2 1/2 cups, (preferably sweeter varieties: honeycrisp, gala, braeburn or winesap), chopped
Optional: 1/2 cup walnuts or pecans, chopped

Combine flours, baking soda, salt and cinnamon in bowl, fold ingredients together with a spoon. With a hand mixer, beat together eggs, sugar and yogurt in separate bowl. Pour wet ingredients into dry ingredients and beat together until all ingredients are incorporated. Fold in apples and nuts with a wooden spoon.

Pour batter into a 9"x 9" baking pan. Bake at 350 degrees for about 40-45 minutes. Test for doneness in the center of the cake with a small thin knife. If knife emerges clean, then cake is done. Cool on a rack for 10- 15 minutes. Serve warm.

Preparation time: 60 minutes (15 minutes to prepare and 45 minutes to cook)
Makes 9 servings

GF Warrior Kitchen and Product Essentials

Whole Grains	**Flours**	**Legumes**	**Condiments**
Brown Rice	*Bob's Red Mill GF*	Adzuki Beans	*San-J* Wheat-free Tamari
Basmati Rice	White Rice	Lentils	*Thai Kitchen* Fish Sauce
Jasmine Rice	Brown Rice	Black beans	Miso paste
Long Grain White Rice	Sorghum	Garbanzo beans	*Eden-brand* umeboshi plum vinegar
Wild Rice	GF Flour Blends	Kidney beans	Cooking sake
Quinoa	Tapioca	Split peas (yellow and green	*Eden-brand* mirin
Buckwheat	Buckwheat	Pinto beans	Balsamic vinegar
Corn	Millet	Cannelini beans	Apple cider vinegar
Amaranth	Corn Flour	Mung beans	Red wine vinegar
Millet	*Arrowhead Mills* Corn Meals (Yellow and Blue)	Black eyed peas	Brown rice vinegar
Tef	Almond Meal	Navy beans	
Bob's Red Mill Certified GF Oats	Chick Pea Flour	Fava beans	

Herbs and Spices	**Fresh Vegetables**	**Fruits**	**Nuts/Seeds/Dried Fruits**
Sea salt	Kale	Apples	Raw cashews
Whole black and mixed peppercorns	Swiss chard	Pears	Roasted almonds
Curry powder	Collard Greens	Pomegranate	Hazelnuts
Turmeric	Broccoli	Oranges	Walnuts
Coriander	Brussel Sprouts	Grapefruit	Pecans
Cinnamon	Zucchini	Lemon and limes	Brazil nuts
Cumin	Wild mushrooms	Peaches	Pistachios
Cloves	Delicata/acorn squash	Blueberries	Flax seeds
Red Chili Flakes	Parsnips	Plums	Sunflower seeds
Chili Powder	Rutabaga	Cherries	Pumpkin seeds
Ground ginger	Turnips	Nectarines	Sesame seeds (black and brown)
Thyme	Tomatoes	Avocado	Chia seeds
Rosemary	Corn	Apricots	Cranberries
Sage	Cauliflower	Papaya	Raisins
Fennel seeds	Red and Green Cabbage	Pineapple	Black Mission Figs
	Beets	Mango	Apricots
	Carrots		Dates
	Celery		Currants
	Potatoes		
	Sea vegetables		
	Garlic		
	Ginger		
	Red and yellow onions		

Meats/Dairy/Eggs	**Oils**	**Sweeteners**	**Other Foods**
Organic, grass-fed, local beef, pastured poultry	Unrefined extra virgin olive oil	Raw honey	Corn tortillas
Cold water fish: halibut, salmon, cod, rockfish, trout, tilapia	Canola oil	Maple syrup	Veggie and chicken broths
Assorted hard cheeses	Coconut oil	Agave nectar	*Tinkyada* Rice Pastas
Whole milk	Toasted sesame oil	Succanat	Canned tomatoes
Plain yogurts	Chili oil	Brown sugar	Rice Crackers
Pastured eggs	Walnut oil	Brown rice syrup	Corn chips
			Coconut, rice, nut milks
			Herbal teas

oduct suggestions are italicized throughout this chart. GF Warrior is not endorsed by products at this time. Warrior product suggestions are based on eir quality, availability and accessibility in local groceries and natural food stores.

Appendices

Gluten-free Grain Power
Budgeting for Gluten-free Diets
The Gluten Sensitivity Spectrum
25 Naturally Gluten-free Snacks
Gluten-free Resources

Appendix A: Gluten-free Grain Power

Incorporating grains into your diet can be challenging if you're gluten-free. Wheat and other gluten containing grains are pervasive in the standard American diet. There are in fact many whole grains that are naturally gluten-free, including the more familiar rice, corn and oats, and the less familiar, millet, buckwheat, quinoa, tef, amaranth, sorghum and montina.

Whole grains are important because they contain all of the nutrients in the grain: fiber, vitamins and minerals, and phytonutrients; whereas refined grains are nutritionally less superior. Nutrients are lost during the refining process because core edible parts of the grain are removed. For example, the germ and bran of a whole wheat kernel are removed in the process of making white flour. That means fiber, B vitamins, essential fatty acids, vitamin E, minerals and protein are all lost in the refining process. The whole grains listed below can be purchased in most natural food stores and in traditional supermarkets.

Amaranth: These tiny brown grains have an unusually high protein content, 18 percent, including high levels of lysine, an essential amino acid. High in iron and calcium and twice the fiber content of wheat. It has a nutty and earthy flavor. The flour can be used for baking and pancakes. The whole grain can be combined with other grains and cooked up as a porridge.

Buckwheat: A misnomer, buckwheat is not part of the wheat family; it is a seed of a weedlike plant related to rhubarb, not a grain. Buckwheat originated in North Central Asia. It can be purchased in different forms, as "groats", roasted (kasha) or unroasted, as flour, and in noodles. Cook up buckwheat as a breakfast gruel, grain pilaf or stuffing. Use the flour in substantial breakfast pancakes and in savory crepes.

Corn: Corn flour, corn meals, polenta, grits and corn tortillas are all staple gluten substitutes. Use corn tortillas in place of bread; corn meal and corn flour in baked products and corn breads. Polenta and corn grits are delicious breakfast cereals.

Millet: Small, yellow, unfortunately found in bird seed mixtures and animal feed in the US, millet is an underutilized, versatile whole grain. Its alkaline nature makes it easy to digest. High in protein, potassium and magnesium, millet can be cooked up as a breakfast porridge, served in salads, soups and stuffings. The flour is a good choice for pancakes, cookies and other baked goods.

Montina (Indian Ricegrass): Not related to rice, Indian Ricegrass is a seed which was once one of the staple foods of Native Americans. Montina®, which is milled from Indian ricegrass, is a tan-colored flour which is high in fiber, protein, vitamins and minerals. It is a registered product, developed at the University of Montana. Montina can be used to replace a portion of other gluten free flours in most recipes to improve texture and nutritional quality.

Oats (Only Certified Gluten-free):** Oats are inherently GF, but usually grown and milled with other gluten-containing grains and therefore, heavily cross-contaminated. In order to be gluten-free friendly, they must be grown in single crop fields, milled in dedicated facilities, and have the Gluten-free Certification, the gold standard for GF product testing which guarantees that the product is GF. Oats are high in soluble fiber, selenium, tryptophan and protein. A piping hot bowl of oatmeal is a nutty and warming breakfast treat. Serve it with nuts, fruits and milk of choice. Use oats in cookies, muffins, stuffings and toppings for crisps.

Quinoa: Pronounced keen-wah, it was first cultivated in South America, 8,000 years ago. The Incas recognized its value in increasing stamina in their warriors. Quinoa is one of the most nutritious whole grains. It contains all of the amino acids, as well as B vitamins, iron, zinc, calcium and vitamin E. It has a nutty and sometimes bitter flavor due to the fact that it's coated with saponin, a naturally occurring bitter substance, which should be washed off before cooking. Quinoa is a versatile grain. Serve it as a morning porridge, a side dish mixed with beans, nuts and seeds, mix with greens, roasted vegetables, or serve with fish or chicken. The flour is wonderful in cookies.

Rice: The grain that feeds the world. Rice comes in all colors, shapes, sizes and textures: white, brown, black, purple, short grain, long grain, wild, basmati, jasmine and arborio. It is the grain that has the second highest worldwide production next to maize (corn). In East Asian cultures, rice is served at every meal. Rice is incredibly versatile and can be combined with legumes, nuts and seeds, fresh vegetables and meats. Serve rice as a sweeter dish in the morning as a porridge or pudding. Use rice flour in baked items and pancakes.

Sorghum: Sweet, neutral flavor, a good gluten-free flour for baking because it mimics the action of wheat flour. Several GF beers are made with fermented sorghum. Try sweet sorghum flour in cake, bread and cookie recipes.

Tef: Native to Ethiopian cultures, these miniscule brown grains are nutritionally superior to other grains, high in minerals such as iron, calcium, potassium and magnesium. If you've dined in Ethiopian restaurants, you've had Tef. Ingera, the flat bread served with food, is made from Tef flour and fermented with a sourdough starter.

** Oats have been a debatable food in the celiac disease community for many years because of cross-contamination issues. The US and Canadian Celiac Disease Associations recommend that celiacs *refrain* from eating oats due to cross-contamination issues. However, there are other US celiac and gluten intolerance organizations that approve consumption of oats for individuals with celiac disease, only if they are *Certified Gluten-Free.* The GF Certification is the gold standard for GF product testing and it guarantees that the product is GF. If you have celiac disease, please make an informed decision about eating oats with your doctor and nutritionist.

Appendix B:
Budgeting for GF Diets: 5 Money Saving Shopping Tips

Gluten-free (GF) diets can be costly. The availability of GF foods in the marketplace is on the rise, however, the market prices of many of these products make them inaccessible to those on a budget. The GF diet is challenging in general to sustain in the long-term, and when you tack on the financial implications, compliance becomes more of an issue. Here are 5 tips to help you economize when grocery shopping.

Find the bulk bins in your supermarket: Foods that are sold in bulk, such as whole grains, nuts and seeds, and dried fruits, are less expensive than their packaged counterparts. Bulk foods usually do not contain gluten or added refined sweeteners, oils, and chemicals. Always defer to the bulk section when you're in need of these foods. For example, 1 pound of bulk rice costs $0.89 at most supermarkets, whereas a 1 pound box of packaged rice is $1.69, almost double the price of bulk.

Caution: Cross-contamination can be an issue in bulk bins. If the bins and scoops are not washed out thoroughly before adding a GF item, there can be risk of cross-contamination. Individuals with celiac must be careful about this and research indicates that the "non-celiac gluten intolerant" should be equally as careful. Always read bin labels. If you see evidence of cross-contamination such as flour dust on or nearby the GF items, report it to the grocery manager. Some stores are more conscious about this than others, exclusively assigning GF and non-GF items to specific bins. When in doubt, inquire with the grocery manager.

Cook with whole grains: There are many whole grains that are naturally gluten-free such as rice, corn, quinoa, millet, buckwheat and teff. Grains are versatile and can be used as the base of a dish such as fried rice, polenta, or kasha. They can also be used in side dishes, salads or served hot with nuts and fruit, as breakfast porridge. Noted above, it is cheaper to purchase whole grains in bulk rather than packaged.

Eat a whole foods diet: When individuals are put on a GF diet, the first question that pops into their minds is "What am I going eat?" Do not panic. The fact is, there are countless whole foods that are naturally GF including: fruits and vegetables, meat, poultry, fish, eggs, cheeses, butter, whole grains noted above, nuts and seeds, soy products, beans, coffees and teas, oils, honey, maple syrup, and spices. It can be more time consuming, but it is less expensive and more nutritious to construct meals using foods in their natural state, whole foods.

Minimize consumption of GF packaged foods: If possible, reduce the frequency with which you purchase GF packaged foods. When purchased in abundance, these foods will inflate your grocery bill. They are enticing because they're "ready-to-go" and it is challenging to find decent GF "ready-to-eat" meals, sweet things, cookies, bars, etc.

However, an abundance of naturally GF whole foods exists and when combined, these foods can make healthy, low cost snacks and meals. See 25 Naturally Gluten-free Snacks for whole food snack ideas.

Get curious about GF baking: GF packaged baked goods and baking mixes can be quite pricey. For example, GF packaged cookies may run $3-6 dollars per box depending on the brand and where you shop. GF cake and bread mixes also run about $4-7 dollars per box. GF baking can be intimidating, even for a seasoned pastry chef. In Philadelphia, there are resources to help you navigate this new world. Whole Foods Market and Essene Market offer GF Baking Classes. Find recipes online and start experimenting with different GF flours such as quinoa, sorghum, rice and bean. Blue and yellow corn meals and nut-based flours also work well in GF baked products. Bob's Red Mill and Arrowhead Mills sell these products certified GF, the gold standard for GF product testing. This certification guarantees that the product is GF.

Appendix C:
The Gluten Sensitivity Spectrum

There are several terms that are used to describe adverse reactions to gluten: celiac disease, gluten intolerance and gluten and wheat allergies. It is important to distinguish between these terminologies for a number of reasons. While the accepted treatment for these conditions is similar, *removal of gluten from one's diet*, the long-term health consequences and medical management are different. Understanding the spectrum of gluten sensitivity will enable you to better understand your condition and access appropriate medical, nutritional and social resources.

Gluten

Gluten is a protein molecule found in wheat, rye and barley. Gluten is found in the majority of bread and baked products, pastas, breakfast cereals and beers. It can also be found in sauces (soy sauce), salad dressings, soups, candies, flavorings, additives, food colorings and many other foods. For the purposes of brevity, an exhaustive list of foods containing gluten is not listed in this book. Please visit the Gluten Intolerance Group of North America http://gluten.net/publications.php for a detailed list.

Celiac Disease

Celiac disease is an autoimmune disorder that affects 1 in 133 individuals in the US or an estimated 1% of Americans. Consumption of gluten triggers celiac disease and initiates an autoimmune response in the body, whereby the surface of the small intestine begins to atrophy. Atrophy of the small intestine causes malabsorption of certain nutrients and consequently nutrient deficiencies. Common symptoms include fatigue, gastrointestinal distress, headaches, dizziness, neurological problems and joint pain. Nutrient malabsorption caused by celiac can result in osteoporosis, iron-deficiency anemia, cancer, diabetes, heart disease and infertility. Celiac is a genetic disease and it runs in families. It can manifest itself at any point in an individual's lifetime. The only treatment that exists for celiac disease is a lifelong adherence to the gluten-free diet.

Gluten Intolerance

Gluten intolerance refers to an adverse reaction following the ingestion of gluten containing products. Gluten intolerance results from the body's inability to digest the gliadin protein fraction in gluten. Individuals who experience this distress but show improvement after adopting a GF diet generally have *non-celiac* gluten intolerance. Adverse reactions in gluten intolerant individuals do not cause damage to the small intestine inherent in celiac disease, however. Gluten intolerance can result from a variety of causes and can affect every system in the body. There are over 200 conditions that are associated with gluten intolerance including irritable bowel syndrome, gas, bloating, diarrhea, constipation, ataxia, migraines, asthma, arthritis, thyroid issues, eczema and respiratory difficulties. What distinguishes celiac disease from gluten intolerance is the atrophy of the small intestine.

Wheat and Gluten Allergies

Wheat and gluten allergies are among the top 8 food sources of allergens in the US (*Top 8 include*: peanuts, tree nuts, milk, eggs, soy, shellfish, fish and wheat). A food allergy can be best explained as a reaction in which the body's immune system overreacts to a food and mistakenly produces antibodies to the food. This reaction is often severe and can occur within minutes to an hour after eating the offending food. Symptoms associated with wheat and gluten allergies include wheezing, skin rashes, lip swelling, hives, diarrhea, nausea and vomiting. The branch of the immune system initiated in allergic reactions is different from the branch involved in the autoimmune reactions of celiac disease.

References:

Gluten Intolerance Group of North America. Gluten Sensitivity: Can Gluten Intolerance Make Me Sick? www.gluten.net/publications.php. Date accessed, November 20, 2010.

Celiac Disease Center at Columbia University. http://www.celiacdiseasecenter.columbia.edu/A_Patients/A02-FAQ.htm. Date accessed, November 24, 2010.

The University of Maryland Celiac Disease Research Center http://www.celiaccenter.org/celiac/faq.asp. Date accessed, November 23, 2010.

The University of Chicago Celiac Disease Center. http://www.celiacdisease.net/factsheets. Date accessed, October 15, 2010.

Center for Food Allergies. www.centerforfoodallergies.com/celiac_disease.htm. Date Accessed, November 10, 2010.

Mayo Clinic. Wheat Allergy. http://www.mayoclinic.com/health/wheat-allergy/DS01002. Date accessed, October 3, 2010.

Green, P., Jones, R. 2006. *Celiac Disease: A Hidden Epidemic.* New York: Harper Collins.

Wangen, S. 2009. *Healthier Without Wheat.* Seattle: Innate Health Publishing.

Appendix D:
25 Naturally Gluten-free Snack Ideas

Finding healthy, grab-and-go snacks can be challenging on a gluten-free diet. Gluten is pervasive in most packaged snack foods. Whole foods that are naturally gluten-free like cheeses, fruits, veggies, nuts and seeds, and grains make wonderful snacks when combined. Listed below are 25 original combinations of GF whole foods to meet your snack needs. These snacks must be constructed by hand. They do not exist in these forms in any supermarket.

1. Corn tortillas with hummus and sprouts
2. Smoked salmon on rice crackers
3. Blue corn chips and salsa fresca
4. Bananas and cashew butter
5. Bosc pears and gruyere
6. Make your own trail mix: raw cashews, raisins, almonds, hazelnuts, dark chocolate chips
7. Plain yogurt with maple syrup, cinnamon, and apple slices
8. Celery sticks and goats chevre
9. Hard-boiled egg with sea salt and crushed black pepper
10. Honey crisp apple slices and peanut butter
11. Dark chocolate squares and fresh strawberries
12. Black bean dip with yellow corn chips
13. Next day rice with crushed nuts, seeds and tamari
14. Fresh blueberries and heavy cream
15. Avocado and cherry tomatoes
16. Canned tuna fish, carrot sticks and sweet pickles
17. Red grapes and swiss cheese
18. Baked sweet potato with ricotta and sautéed chard or spinach
19. Cottage cheese with peaches
20. Warm corn tortillas with smoked salmon, tahini and greens
21. Cashews and hazelnuts
22. Cream cheese spread on *Mary's Gone* flax crackers
23. Sliced deli meat and avocado on a brown rice tortilla
24. *Van's* whole grain GF waffle with honey and hazelnut butter
25. Air popped popcorn mixed with crushed dried nori, garlic salt and pepper

Appendix E: Gluten-free Resources

Philadelphia Area Restaurants:
Bindi (bindibyob.com/bindi) – Philadelphia, PA (Indian)
Bonefish Grill (bonefishgrill.com) - Willow Grove, PA; Newtown Square, PA; Exton, PA; Marlton, NJ; Deptford, NJ; Egg Harbor Township, NJ (seafood)
Buddakan (buddakan.com) – Philadelphia, PA; Atlantic City, NJ (pan-Asian)
Casona (mycasona.com) – Collingswood, NJ (Latin/Cuban)
Giorgio on Pine (giorgioonpine.com) –Philadelphia, PA (Italian)
Horizons (horizonsphiladelphia.com) - Philadelphia, PA (vegan)
Iron Hill Brewery & Restaurant (ironhillbrewery.com) - Media, PA; North Wales, PA; Phoenixville, PA; West Chester, PA; Maple Shade, NJ; Newark, DE; Wilmington, DE (American)
The Melting Pot (meltingpot.com) - King of Prussia, PA; Philadelphia, PA; Warrington, PA; Atlantic City, NJ; Wilmington, DE (fondue)
Mumbai Bistro (mumbaibistro.com) – Philadelphia, PA (Indian)
P.F.Chang's China Bistro (pfchangs.com) - Collegeville, PA; Plymouth Meeting, PA; Warrington, PA; Glen Mills, PA; Marlton, NJ; Princeton, NJ; Atlantic City, NJ (pan-Asian)
Pei Wei Asian Diner (peiwei.com) - Philadelphia (Main Line), PA; Springfield, PA; Cherry Hill, NJ; Moorestown, NJ (pan-Asian)
Seasons 52 Fresh Grill (seasons52.com) – King of Prussia, PA; Cherry Hill, NJ (Contemporary American)

Philadelphia Area Markets:
Big Bear Natural Foods (bigbearnaturalfoods.com) - Langhorne, PA; Morrisville, PA; Ewing, NJ; Pennington, NJ
Food For All Market (foodforallmarket.com) - Philadelphia, PA
Gluten Free Dynasty (glutenfreedynasty.com) - Pennsauken, NJ
Kimberton Whole Foods (kimbertonwholefoods.com) - Douglasville, PA; Downingtown, PA; Kimberton, PA; Ottsville, PA
Martindale's Natural Market (martindalesnutritionl.com) - Springfield, PA
Trader Joe's (traderjoes.com) - Ardmore, PA; Media, PA; Philadelphia, PA; Wayne, PA; Jenkintown, PA; North Wales, PA; Marlton, NJ; West Windsor, NJ; Wilmington, DE
Wegmans (wegmans.com) - Collegeville, PA; Downingtown, PA; Malvern, PA; Warrington, PA; Cherry Hill, NJ; Mt. Laurel, NJ; West Windsor, NJ
Whole Foods Market (wholefoods.com) - Philadelphia, PA (2); Jenkintown, PA; Wynnewood, PA; Devon, PA; North Wales, PA; Plymouth Meeting, PA; Marlton, NJ; Princeton, NJ
Weaver's Way Co-op – weaverway.coop - Mt. Airy and Chestnut Hill, Philadelphia, PA
Restaurants and markets section reprinted with permission from GlutenfreePhilly http://www.glutenfreephilly.com.

National Resources
Gluten Intolerance Group of North America
www.gluten.net

Canadian Celiac Disease Association
www.celiac.ca

National Foundation for Celiac Awareness
www.celiaccentral.org

About the Author

Genevieve Sherrow is a recent graduate of the Master's Nutrition Program at Bastyr University, a private, accredited institution in Seattle, Washington internationally known for its programs in the natural health sciences. Her nutrition articles and original recipes have appeared in the *Seattle Post Intelligencer*'s online natural medicine column and in Bastyr University's print and web publications such as *Health E – News* and *Healthy and Wise*. She also writes for her own blog, Nourishing Foods, on the nutritional, medicinal and culinary applications of whole foods.

Genevieve enjoys designing therapeutic diets to manage symptoms associated with chronic illnesses. She believes in the application of low allergen and anti-inflammatory diets for individuals affected by autoimmune and dermatological conditions, obesity and psychological disorders. She also utilizes Ayurvedic and Traditional Chinese Medicine approaches to nutrition in her clinical work. Genevieve gained invaluable clinical experience as a student clinician at the Bastyr Center for Natural Health, the teaching clinic of Bastyr University, where she provided nutritional counseling to patients affected by diabetes, cancer, heart disease, food allergies and obesity.

Genevieve was diagnosed with gluten intolerance in 2007, and since then has been an advocate and community educator for individuals affected by celiac disease, gluten intolerance and other food allergies. She has worked with the Gluten Intolerance Group of North America, the IBS Treatment Center, Innate Health Foundation and the Puget Sound Co-op Cooking Education Program. She was a lead organizer for Celiac Disease Awareness Month at Bastyr University in 2009.

If you enjoyed what you read here, *Gluten-free Warrior* is accepting donations for self-publishing efforts. If you would like to donate to *Gluten-free Warrior*, please contact Genevieve Sherrow at **215-694-7931** or **glutenfreewarrior@gmail.com.** *Gluten-free Warrior* is also available for hire for food and recipe writing projects, gluten-free and food allergy education, counseling, cooking and consulting.

For more information about gluten-free whole foods nutrition and cooking, visit:

Nourishing Foods:
http://wholefoodreflections.blogspot.com

Gluten-free Warrior:
http://gfwarrior.blogspot.com